M000198536

SHAMBHALA LIBRARY

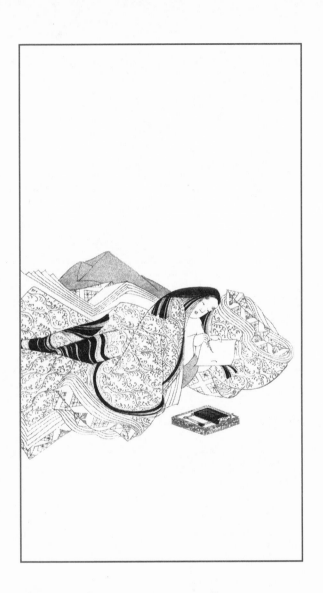

Love Poems

FROM THE JAPANESE

translated by
KENNETH REXROTH

edited by
Sam Hamill

SHAMBHALA
Boston & London
2003

Shambhala Publications, Inc.
Horticultural Hall
300 Massachusetts Avenue
Boston, Massachusetts 02115
www.shambhala.com

Published by arrangement with New Directions Publishing
Corporation, 80 Eighth Avenue, New York, NY 10011

9 8 7 6 5 4 3 2 1

PRINTED IN GERMANY
∞ This edition is printed on acid-free paper that meets
the American National Standards Institute z39.48 Standard.
Distributed in the United States by Random House, Inc.,
and in Canada by Random House of Canada Ltd

Library of Congress Cataloging-in-Publication Data
Love poems from the Japanese/Kenneth Rexroth [compiler];
edited by Sam Hamill.—1st Shambhala library ed.
p.   cm.—(Shambhala library)
Previously published as Shambhala pocket classics in 1994.
ISBN 1-57062-976-5
1. Waka—Translations into English.   2. Love poetry,
Japanese—Translations into English.   I. Rexroth, Kenneth,
1905–   II. Hamill, Sam.   III. Series.
PL782.E3 L68   2003
895.6'100803543—dc21
2002026916

CONTENTS

EDITOR'S INTRODUCTION

Kenneth Rexroth's *One Hundred Poems from the Japanese* (New Directions, 1955) introduced a generation of readers to a poetry of great subtlety and sensibility and, through four decades and three subsequent collections of Japanese poetry in translation, he left an indelible print on American culture. Prized for their precision and transparency, Rexroth's Japanese translations have introduced many young readers to poetry in general, have been presented as gifts from lover to lover and friend to friend, and have been imitated by poets at least since Jack Kerouac's haiku and Robert Bly's *Silence in the Snowy Field* (Wesleyan University Press, 1962).

In his brilliant introduction to *One Hundred Poems from the Japanese,* Rexroth reminds his readers that the opening lines of a *tanka,* the traditional five-line Japanese poem, often serve only to "create a setting" for the closure, and as a kind of preface "have only an emotional or metaphoric relevance, and introduce into a poem of only thirty-one syllables an element of dissociation." Scores of American poets explored just such a structure in short lyrical poems in the sixties and seventies, from the luminous dark poems and translations of W. S. Merwin to the flat, pseudo-mystical phrases of mere imitators.

In his essay "The Influence of Classical Japanese Poetry" (*The Elastic Retort,* Seabury Press, 1973), Rexroth offers this warning for readers of poetry in translation: "If Japanese, or for that matter, Chinese poetry is translated into Western syntax and all the spark gaps of meaning are filled up, what results is a series of logically expressed epigrams, usually sentimental, with a vulgar little moral interpretation attached, or at the best a metaphorical epigram of a moment of sensibility like [Ezra] Pound's 'In a Station of the Metro,' which most resembles, not classical Japanese *tanka* or even the best *haiku,* but the more sentimental work of the late Yeddo [Edo] period. It is this compulsion to fill up the gaps and interpret the poem for Western readers which vitiates the work of so many translators, both Western and Japanese. They too often believe that Westerners could not possibly understand a Japanese poem in all its simplicity."

But the apparent "simplicity" of classical Japanese poetry, especially the five-line tanka, the staple of Rexroth's four hundred-odd poems translated from Japanese, is often an illusion. Like the classical Chinese poets they emulated and closely studied, Japanese poets filled their poems with slightly altered lines from "the classics" and referential metaphors and similes. Willis Hawley, one of Ezra Pound's principal informants on all things Chinese, once offered the left-handed compliment, "He knows when to dumb it down," meaning that Pound didn't try to fill in all the "spark gaps" of allusion as he translated.

Rexroth, especially in his longer philosophical poems, engages in a practice similar to that of Pound's "ideographic method" in *The Cantos,* a layering achieved by allusion and echo and paraphrase as well as by direct quotation. Part Three of the title poem to *The Phoenix and the Tortoise* (New Directions, 1944) begins:

> *Softly and singly an owl*
> *Cries in my sleep. I awake and turn*
> *My head, but there is only the moon*
> *Sinking in the early dawn.*

Substituting an owl for a Japanese cuckoo, this is a translation of a famous poem by Gotoku Daiji. This and several other instances of Rexroth's personal use of whole Japanese poems within his own have been traced by Sanehide Kodama in *American Poetry and Japanese Culture* (Archon Books, 1984).

Having spent much of his life absorbing Asian literary culture in general and Buddhist culture in particular, Rexroth was entirely comfortable writing poems as infused with the spirit of Buddhist dharma as any of those he translated, and this is obvious in his later work, especially in *The Morning Star* (New Directions, 1979), which includes a longer poem, "On Flower Wreath Hill," the name of which means *cemetery* in Chinese and Japanese. This meditation on his own temporality, written while Rexroth was living in Kyoto in 1974–75, makes free use of many classical Japanese poems, so that Rexroth's own sense of passing is connected directly with the poetry and poets of a thousand years ago.

His invention of "a contemporary young woman who lives near the temple of Marishi-ben in Kyoto," Marichiko, is an audacious stroke of genius replete with echoes of Buddhist sutras and of China's greatest woman poet, Li Ch'ing-chao, whom Rexroth was then translating with Ling Chung. In some way, perhaps, one might say of Rexroth that he became "feminized" in sensibility late in his life—through translating women poets of China and Japan in addition to the above.

Throughout a long and difficult life, Kenneth Rexroth believed in an idealized love in which passion, compassion, and spiritual enlightenment become inevitable. He was fond of saying, when it was still considered indecent to mention such things in mixed company, "Sexual love is one of the greatest forms of contemplation." He was one of this century's great poets of erotic love in part because he believed erotic love to be the physical manifestation of spiritual devotion, an attitude informed by Vedantic and Buddhist philosophy.

In his translations of classical Japanese love poems in particular, Rexroth brings a deep philosophical kinship into harmony with a profoundly romantic intu-ition and achieves an apparent simplicity not at all at odds with the original. He makes an American English equivalent that finds resonance in the most enduring, complex, and fundamental human experience.

These poems have been selected from *One Hundred Poems from the Japanese* (New Directions, 1955); *One Hundred More Poems from the Japanese* (New Directions, 1976); *The Burning Heart* (Seabury Press, 1977), republished as *Women Poets of Japan* (New Directions, 1982); and *Love Poems of Marichiko* (Christopher's Books, 1978). The "Notes on the Poets" have been adapted from material in these same publications.

— SAM HAMILL

Love Poems from the Japanese

I loathe the twin seas
Of being and not being
And long for the mountain
Of bliss untouched by
The changing tides.

—ANONYMOUS, *Manyōshū*

Her bracelets tinkle

Her anklets clink

She sways at her clattering loom

She hurries to have a new

Obi ready when he comes.

—Anonymous, *Manyōshū*

On Komochi Mountain

From the time the young leaves
   sprout
Until they turn red
I think I would like to sleep with you
What do you think of that?

—Anonymous, *Manyōshū*

Shall we stay in the
House to make love, when over
The grasses of Inami Moor
There glows the moonfilled night?

—Anonymous, *Manyōshū*

I do not care if

Our love making is exposed

As the rainbow over

The Yasaka dam at Ikaho

If only I can suck and suck you.

—ANONYMOUS, *Manyōshū*

When I pick up my koto
A cry of sorrow comes from it.
Is it possible that
In the koto's hollow
My wife's spirit
Has secluded itself?

— ANONYMOUS, *Manyōshū*

Over the reeds the
Twilight mists rise and settle.
The wild ducks cry out
As the evening turns cold.
Lover, how I long for you.

—ANONYMOUS FRONTIER
GUARD, *Manyōshū*

In the dusk

The road is hard to see.

Wait 'till moonrise,

So I can watch you go.

— Oyakeme, A Girl of
Buzen, *Manyōshū*

In the empty mountains
The leaves of the bamboo grass
Rustle in the wind.
I think of a girl
Who is not here.

—KAKINOMOTO NO HITOMARO

When I gathered flowers

For my girl

From the top of the plum tree

The lower branches

Drenched me with dew.

—Kakinomoto no Hitomaro

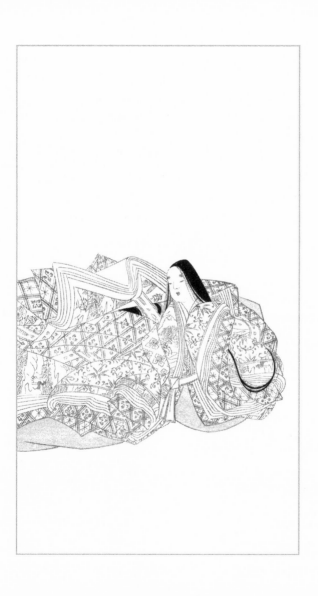

Gossip grows like weeds
In a summer meadow.
My girl and I
Sleep arm in arm.

—Kakinomoto no Hitomaro

In the Autumn mountains
The colored leaves are falling.
If I could hold them back,
I could still see her.

— Kakinomoto no Hitomaro

This morning I will not

Comb my hair.

It has lain

Pillowed on the hand of my lover.

—Kakinomoto no Hitomaro

Your hair has turned white
While your heart stayed
Knotted against me.
I shall never
Loosen it now.

— Kakinomoto no Hitomaro

The colored leaves
Have hidden the paths
On the autumn mountain.
How can I find my girl,
Wandering on ways I do not know?

—Kakinomoto no Hitomaro

I sit at home

In our room

By our bed

Gazing at your pillow.

— KAKINOMOTO NO HITOMARO

I waited for my
Lover until I could hear
In the night the oars of the boat
Crossing the River of Heaven.

— Kakinomoto no Hitomaro

When I left my girl

In her grave on Mount Hikite

And walked down the mountain path,

I felt as though I were dead.

— Kakinomoto no Hitomaro

My girl is waiting for me

And does not know

That my body will stay here

On the rocks of Mount Kamo.

— Kakinomoto no Hitomaro

Bound up it always
Came undone.
Unbound it was so long.
Now that I have not
Been with you for days
Is your hair all done up?

— Mikata Shami

Everybody tells me

My hair is too long

I leave it

As you saw it last

Dishevelled by your hands.

— LADY SONO NO OMI IKUHA
(Mikata's wife)

25

You say, "I will come."

And you do not come.

Now you say, "I will not come."

So I shall expect you.

Have I learned to understand you?

— Lady Ōtomo no Sakanoe

Better never to have met you
In my dream
Than to wake and reach
For hands that are not there.

— ŌTOMO NO YAKAMOCHI
(*to Lady Sakanoe*)

I will come to you
Through the ford at Saho,
The plovers piping about me
As my horse wades
The clear water.

— ŌTOMO NO YAKAMOCHI

When I see the first
New moon, faint in the twilight,
I think of the moth eyebrows
Of a girl I saw only once.

— Ōtomo no Yakamochi

We were together
Only a little while,
And we believed our love
Would last a thousand years.

— Ōtomo no Yakamochi

To love somebody
Who doesn't love you,
Is like going to a temple
And worshipping the behind
Of a wooden statue
Of a hungry devil.

— LADY KASA

I wish I were close
To you as the wet skirt of
A salt girl to her body.
I think of you always.

—Yamabe no Akahito

The years have touched me.
I worry that I grow frail with age.
But I only need to see
Your flower like beauty
For all anxiety and heaviness
To leave me.

— Fujiwara no Yoshifusa

Without changing color
in the emptiness
of this world of ours,
the heart of man
fades like a flower.

— ONO NO KOMACHI

You do not come

On this moonless night.

I wake wanting you.

My breasts heave and blaze.

My heart burns up.

—ONO NO KOMACHI

Doesn't he realize

that I am not

like the swaying kelp

in the surf,

where the seaweed gatherer

can come as often as he wants.

— Ono no Komachi

I fell asleep thinking of him,
and he came to me.
If I had known it was only a dream
I would never have awakened.

—Ono no Komachi

Following the roads
Of dream to you, my feet
Never rest. But one glimpse of you
In reality would be
Worth all these many nights of love.

—ONO NO KOMACHI

Since "the pillow knows all"
we slept without a pillow.
Still my reputation
reaches to the skies
like a dust storm.

— LADY ISE

Even in dreams
I do not want him to know
that it is me he is making love to,
for I am overcome with blushes
when I see my face in the morning
  mirror.

—LADY ISE

Your fine promises
Were like the dew of life
To a parched plant,
But now the autumn
Of another year goes by.

— Prince Fujiwara no
Motoyoshi

I am unhappy.

I do not care what happens.

I must see you, even

If it means I shall

Be lost in Naniwa Bay.

—Prince Fujiwara no
    Motoyoshi

In the Bay of Sumi

The waves crowd on the beach.

Even in the night

By the corridors of dreams,

I come to you secretly.

— Fujiwara no Toshiyuki

Yoshino River
Flows between Imo Mountain
And Mount Se. All the
World's illusion
Flows between lover and lover.

—Anonymous, *Kokinshū*

When,

Heart overwhelmed with love,

I hurried through the winter night

To the home of my beloved,

The wind on the river was so cold

The plovers cried out in pain.

— KI NO TSURAYUKI

She said she would come
At once, and so I waited
Till the moon rose
In the October dawn.

— MONK SOSEI

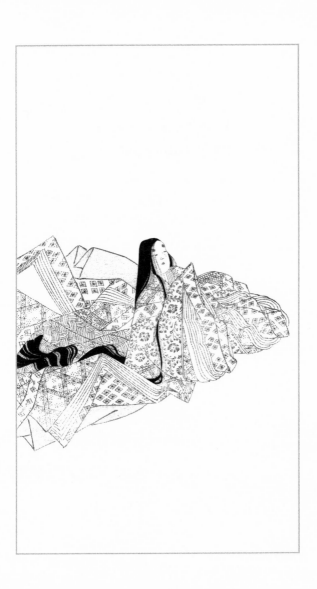

In a gust of wind the white dew

On the autumn grass

Scatters like a broken necklace.

— Bunya no Asayasu

I think of the days
Before I met her
When I seemed to have
No troubles at all.

—Fujiwara no Atsutada

Someone passes,
And while I wonder
If it is he,
The midnight moon
Is covered with clouds.

— Lady Murasaki Shikibu

Since I left her,
Frigid as the setting moon,
There is nothing I loathe
As much as the light
Of dawn on the clouds.

— Mibu no Tadamine

Yes, I am in love.
They were talking about me
Before daylight,
Although I began to love
Without knowing it.

— Mibu no Tadami

Like Michinoku

Cloth, printed with tangled ferns,

My mind is disordered

Because of you,

But my love is not.

— MINAMOTO NO TŌRU

Is our love over?

If only I could ask of your phantom

reflected on the surface

of the pond we made

as a symbol of our love—

but the surface is covered with

duckweed.

—Mother of Michitsuna

Although I hide it
My love shows in my face
So plainly that he asks me,
"Are you thinking of something?"

— Taira no Kanemori

From Mount Arima,

over the bamboo plains of Ina,

the wind blows

rustling the leaves.

How shall I ever forget him?

— DAINI NO SANMI

It is already so late at night
for our meeting,
but it is melancholy not to pause
at the ford of Saho
to listen to the plovers crying.

—ISE TAYŪ

The pillow that knows all
won't tell, for it doesn't know,
and don't you tell
of our dream of a spring night.

— LADY IZUMI SHIKIBU

I picked an azalea
And brought it home.
Now when I contemplate it,
In its crimson dye
I see the color
Of my lover's robe.

— LADY IZUMI SHIKIBU

It is the time of rain and snow

I spend sleepless nights

And watch the frost

Frail as your love

Gather in the dawn.

— LADY IZUMI SHIKIBU

In the dusk the path

You used to come to me

Is overgrown and indistinguishable,

Except for the spider webs

That hang across it

Like threads of sorrow.

— Lady Izumi Shikibu

Will I cease to be,
Or will I remember
Beyond the world,
Our last meeting together?

—Lady Izumi Shikibu

In love longing

I listen to the monk's bell.

I will never forget you

even for an interval

short as those between the

bell notes.

— LADY IZUMI SHIKIBU
*(Written at the sutra chanting
for her dead daughter)*

It would have been better that I slept

the whole night through

without waiting for him,

than to have watched

until the setting of the moon.

— LADY AKAZOME EMON

I should not have waited.
It would have been better
To have slept and dreamed,
Than to have watched night pass,
And this slow moon sink.

— LADY AKAZOME EMON

That spring night I spent
Pillowed on your arm
Never really happened
Except in a dream.
Unfortunately I am
Talked about anyway.

— Lady Suo

Will he always love me?
I cannot read his heart.
This morning my thoughts
Are as disordered
As my black hair.

—LADY HORIKAWA

You do not come, and I wait

On Matsuo beach,

In the calm of evening.

And like the blazing

Water, I too am burning.

— Fujiwara no Sadaie

Why should I be bitter
About someone who was
A complete stranger
Until a certain moment
In a day that has passed.

— Saigyō

Life, like a thread piercing
    through jewels,
if you must break,
break now!
If I live any longer
I will weaken and show my
    hidden love.

—PRINCESS SHIKISHI

I slept in the past,

that will never come back,

as though it was the present.

Around my pillow in my dreams

the perfume of orange blossoms

   floated,

like the fragrance of the sleeves

of the man who is gone.

— Princess Shikishi

From the beginning
I knew meeting could only
End in parting, yet
I ignored the coming dawn
And I gave myself to you.

— FUJIWARA NO TEIKA

As the season changes,
I change my clothes
to clothes dyed the color of
    cherry blossoms
which will fade as easily
from the hearts of men.

— SHUNZEI'S DAUGHTER

How can I complain
that you have shaved your hair?
Since I can never again
pull your heartstrings
like a catalpa wood bow,
I have become a nun
following your Way.

—Yokobue

Who knows

that in the depth of the ravine

of the mountain of my hidden heart

a firefly of my love is aflame.

— Abutsu-Ni

We dressed each other
Hurrying to say farewell
In the depth of night.
Our drowsy thighs touched and we
Were caught in bed by the dawn.

— Empress Eifuku

Cats making love in the temple
But people would blame
A man and wife for mating in such
   a place.

— Kawai Chigetsu-Ni

I leave all the scarlet flowers

For the woman I love

And hiding my tears from her

I pick

The flower of forgetfulness.

— Yamakawa Tomiko

I shall hide myself
within the moon of the spring night,
after I have dared to reveal
my love to you.

— Chino Masako

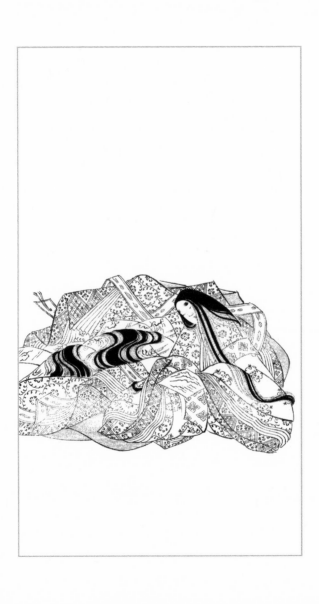

At the beginning
Of the night the whispering
Snow fell, and now stars
Fill this world below on the
Disheveled hair about my face.

—Yosano Akiko

Once, far over the breakers,

I caught a glimpse

Of a white bird

And fell in love

With this dream which obsesses me.

— Yosano Akiko

Hair unbound, in this
Hothouse of lovemaking,
Perfumed with lilies,
I dread the oncoming of
The pale rose of the end of night.

— Yosano Akiko

Amidst the notes
Of my koto is another
Deep mysterious tone,
A sound that comes from
Within my own breast.

— Yosano Akiko

He tempted me to
Come in to say goodbye.
I hesitated to respond
And he brushed my hand away.
But yet—the smell of his clothes
In the soft darkness.

—Yosano Akiko

Not speaking of the way,
Not thinking of what comes after,
Not questioning name or fame,
Here, loving love,
You and I look at each other.

— Yosano Akiko

That evening when
You went away the two of
Us wrote together
On a pillar a poem
About a white clover.

— YOSANO AKIKO

This autumn will end.

Nothing can last forever.

Fate controls our lives.

Fondle my living breasts

With your strong hands.

— YOSANO AKIKO

I can give myself to her

In her dreams

Whispering her own poems

In her ear as she sleeps beside me.

— Yosano Akiko

Without a word
Without a demand
A man and two women
Bowed and parted company
On the sixth of the month.

—Yosano Akiko

Last autumn

The three of us tossed acorns

To the scattering carp.

Now in the cold morning wind off

   the pond

He and I stand hand in chilling hand.

            — YOSANO AKIKO

I have the delusion
that you are with me
as I walk through the fields
of flowers, under the moon.

—Yosano Akiko

Press my breasts,
Part the veil of mystery,
A flower blooms there,
Crimson and fragrant.

—Yosano Akiko

Sweet and sad
like love overwhelmed
with long sighs,
out of the depths of the willow
little by little
the moon appears.

— Yosano Akiko

Come at last to this point
I look back on my passion
And realize that I
Have been like a blind man
Who is unafraid of the dark.

—Yosano Akiko

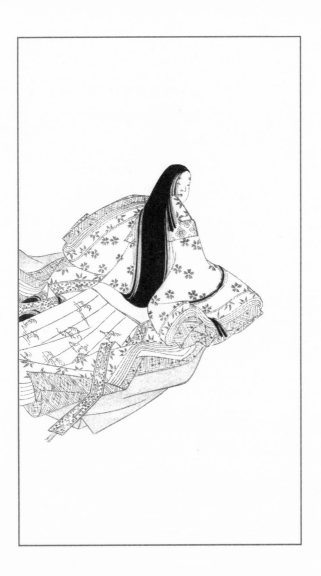

Who is there? Me.

Me who? I am me, you are you.

But you take my pronoun,

And we are us.

— MARICHIKO

I hold your head tight
Between my thighs and press
Against your mouth and
Float away forever in
An orchid boat
On the River of Heaven.

— Marichiko

I cannot forget
The perfumed dusk inside the
Tent of my black hair
As we woke to make love
After a long night of love.

— MARICHIKO

How long, long ago.
By the bridge at Uji,
In our little boat,
We swept through clouds of fireflies.

— MARICHIKO

Making love with you
Is like drinking sea water.
The more I drink
The thirstier I become,
Until nothing can slake my thirst
But to drink the entire sea.

— MARICHIKO

You wake me,
Part my thighs, and kiss me.
I give you the dew
Of the first morning of the world.

— MARICHIKO

Your tongue thrums and moves
Into me, and I become
Hollow and blaze with
Whirling light, like the inside
Of a vast expanding pearl.

— Marichiko

Love me. At this moment we
Are the happiest
People in the world.

— MARICHIKO

Spring is early this year.
Laurel, plums, peaches,
Almonds, mimosa,
All bloom at once. Under the
Moon, night smells like your body.

— Marichiko

Night without end. Loneliness.
The wind has driven a maple leaf
Against the shoji. I wait, as in the
    old days,
In our secret place, under the
    full moon.
The last bell crickets sing.
I found your old love letters,
Full of poems you never published.
Did it matter? They were only
    for me.

— MARICHIKO

Some day in six inches of
Ashes will be all
That's left of our passionate minds,
Of all the world created
By our love, its origin
And passing away.

— MARICHIKO

I wish I could be
Kannon of the thousand heads
To kiss you and Kannon
Of the thousand arms
To embrace you, and
Dainichi to hold you
Forever.

— MARICHIKO

A single ray in the dawn,
The bliss of our love
Is incomprehensible.
No sun shines there, no
Moon, no stars, no lightning flash,
Not even lamplight.
All things are incandescent
With love which lights up all
    the world.

— MARICHIKO

NOTES ON THE POETS

ABUTSU-NI was Maid of Honor to the Princess Kuni-Naishinnō and then the wife of Fujiwara Tameie, the son of the great poet Sadaie, who was the son of the equally great poet Toshinari, called Teika. She was thus part of the late twelfth and early thirteenth century revolution of the sensibilities, the last great moment of classical Japanese poetry. In 1277 she went from Kyoto to Kamakura for a lawsuit regarding the inheritance for herself and Tameie's sons and wrote a diary of her journey, the *Izayoi Nikki,* one of the classics of Japanese prose.

YAMABE NO AKAHITO lived during the reign of the Emperor Shōmu, 734–748 CE. He is thought to have died in 736. He seems to have been in close personal attendance to the Emperor and to have accompanied him on his progresses through the country. His short poems are considered nearly the equal of Hitomaro's, but the latter's *naga uta,* "long poems," are superior. He is a *kasei,* a deified poet.

LADY AKAZOME EMON (?–1027) was the daughter of Taira no Kanemori, the poet and statesman, and the wife of Ōe no Masahira. She was Lady in Waiting to Rinko, the wife of the great minister (Kampaku) Michinaga. She is a later member of the great group of women poets, roughly contemporary with Murasaki and the author of the *Eiga-Monogatari,* the story of the supremacy of the Fujiwara, an unusual type of book for a Japanese woman to write at any time.

YOSANO AKIKO (1878–1942) was the daughter of Ōtori, a merchant in the ancient trading city of Sakai, now absorbed into the Ōsaka metropolitan area. She graduated from Sakai Girls' High School and in 1900 went to Tokyo, studied poetry with Yosano Hiroshi (Tekkan), who considered himself the leader of the new *waka* poetry (*tanka*) movement, and soon married him. For a while, in Tokyo and Kyoto they were involved in a tragic *maison à trois* with a young woman, Yamakawa Tomiko, whom they both loved deeply. After a few years Tomiko died of tuberculosis. Akiko and Hiroshi founded the "New Poetry Society" and its organ, the magazine *Myōjō,* "Morning Star." Hiroshi always thought of himself as the genius of the family, although he was a sentimental and commonplace poet who learned little from the French Symbolists whom he adored. Akiko was quickly recognized and earned enough money to send Hiroshi to Paris from 1911 to 1914, but she was only able to save enough money for herself to stay part of 1912, and members of her family assisted them both to return to Japan. She wrote many collections of poetry, novels, essays, children's stories, and fairy tales. She is the only truly great poet to write in traditional *tanka* form in modern times.

BUNYA NO ASAYASU lived about 900 during the reign of the Emperor Daigo. He is the son of Bunya no Yasuhide, whose poetry I have found untranslatable. Asayasu's poem was written at the request of the Emperor during a garden party and poem-writing contest.

FUJIWARA NO ATSUTADA is believed to have died in 961 CE. He was a *Chūnagon,* a state adviser, and the son of the *Udaijin,* the Minister of the Right of the Emperor Daigo. The Fujiwara family, or rather, clan, still extant and powerful today, is one of the most extraordinary that has ever existed. For centuries they have provided Japan with administrators, regents, Shōguns, poets, generals, painters, philosophers, and abbots.

CHINO MASAKO (1880–1946) was born in Ōsaka, graduated from Women's University in Tokyo, and was married to Chino Shōshō, a poet and professor of German. She visited Europe and became a professor at Women's University.

DAINI NO SANMI (tenth–eleventh century) was the daughter of Murasaki Shikibu, and is known by her rank of honor, the Third Sanmi, and the title of her father or husband, Daini. Women in the Heian Period were seldom known by personal names. It is not true that they did not have them, but the failure to use them is the survival of primitive taboos.

Black hair

Tangled in a thousand strands.

Tangled my hair and

Tangled my tangled memories

Of our long nights of lovemaking.

—Yosano Akiko

EIFUKU MON-IN (1271–1342) was the wife of the Emperor Fushimi. Her personal name was Akiko.

KAKINOMOTO NO HITOMARO flourished in the later years of the seventh century and reputedly died in 739. He was probably a personal attendant of the Emperor Mommu (697–707) and later retired to Iwami where he may have been born, and died there, although his reputed tomb is at Ichii no Moto in Yamato. He is considered Japan's greatest poet and has provided models for countless poems since his time.

LADY HORIKAWA is known only as the *Mon in,* attendant, of the Empress Dowager Taiken, in the middle of the twelfth century.

LADY ISE (tenth century) was the daughter of Fujiwara no Tsugikage, Lord of Ise, later Lord of Yamato. She was the lover of Prince Atsuyoshi, by whom she bore a daughter, the poet Nakatsukasa. She later became a concubine of the Emperor Uda, to whom she bore Prince Yuki-Akari. She is to be distinguished from Ise Tayū, daughter of the Chief Priest of the Ise Shrines, and from the Priestess of Ise who had a brief love affair and an exchange of poems with the poet Narihara in the tenth century.

ISE TAYŪ (eleventh century) was the daughter of Ōnakatomi no Sukechika, the chief priest of the Ise Shrine.

LADY IZUMI SHIKIBU lived at the end of the tenth and the beginning of the eleventh century, a contemporary of Akazome, Murasaki, Sei Shōnagon, and Ise Tayū. She was the daughter of Ōe no Masamune, and the wife of Tachibana no Michisada, the Lord of Izumi, the mistress of Prince Tametaka and his brother Prince Atsumichi, the wife of Fujiwara no Yasumasa, Lord of Tango. Her correspondence with her lover (except the verse, possibly apocryphal) the *Izumi Shikibu Monogatari,* is a masterpiece of Japanese prose. Of all the poets of the classical period, she has, to my mind, the deepest and most poignant Buddhist sensibility.

TAIRA NO KANEMORI flourished in the tenth century. Nothing else is known of him. The Tairas were the third great family of Japan.

LADY KASA lived in the eighth century, and was a lover of Yakamochi. She was possibly related to the family of Kasa Kanamura, who made a collection of poetry, some of which was included in the *Manyōshū,* or to the Monk Manzei, whose secular name was Kasamaro, also a poet of the *Manyōshū.*

KAWAI CHIGETSU-NI (1632–1736) was born in Ōtsu on Lake Ōmi. She was the pupil of Bashō and the mother of the poet Otokuni.

ONO NO KOMACHI (834–880) is the legendary beauty of Japan, comparable to the Chinese Yang Kuei-fei. She was the daughter of Yoshisada, Lord of Dewa.

She is supposed to have died old, ugly, and a beggar, but this is a legend, perpetuated by three of the finest Noh plays. She is certainly one of Japan's "six greatest poets." Her beauty may be legendary but her rank as one of the greatest erotic poets in any language is not. Her poems begin the extreme verbal complexity which distinguishes the poetry of the *Kokinshū Anthology* from the presentational immediacy of the *Manyōshū*

MARICHIKO is the pen name of a contemporary young woman who lives near the temple of Marishiben in Kyoto. Marishi-ben is an Indian, pre-Aryan goddess of the dawn who is a bodhisattva in Buddhism and patron of geisha, prostitutes, women in childbirth, and lovers. Few temples or shrines to her or even statues exist in Japan, but her presence is indicated by statues, often in avenues like sphinxes, of wild boars, who draw her chariot. She has three faces: the front of compassion; one side, a sow; the other a woman in orgasm. She is a popular, though hidden deity of tantric, Tachigawa Shingon, and as the Light of Lights, the *shakti,* the Power of Bliss of Vairocana (the primordial Buddha, Dainichi Nyorai), seated on his lap in sexual bliss.*

MOTHER OF MICHITSUNA is known only by this name or as the wife of the regent Kaneie. She lived at the end of the tenth century at the beginning of the

*See editor's introduction.

great blossoming of women poets, some years earlier than Izumi Shikibu.

MIKATA SHAMI may have been Yamada Mikata who flourished in the seventh and eighth centuries, possibly a contemporary of Hitomaro. He also wrote some Chinese poems.

PRINCE FUJIWARA NO MOTOYOSHI was the son of the Emperor Yōsei, who reigned from 877 to 884.

LADY MURASAKI SHIKIBU lived from 974 to 1031. She is the greatest figure in Japanese literature, the author of *The Tale of Genji,* one of the world's greatest books, of a diary, and of numerous poems. She was the daughter of Tametoki, Lord of Echigo, the granddaughter of Fujiwara no Kanesuke, a well-known poet, and the second wife of Fujiwara no Nobutaka. She was a Lady-in-Waiting to the Empress Akiko. Shikibu is a title, actually a military one, which seems to have been given to important women of the court as a courtesy. Murasaki is the name of the wife of Genji in her novel.

LADY SONO NO OMI IKUHA. Nothing is known of her except that she was Mikata's wife and Sono Ikuha's daughter.

OYAKEME, A GIRL OF BUZEN. Nothing is known of her. Her poem appears in the *Manyōshū* in a group of otherwise unknown young women.

FUJIWARA NO SADAIE lived from 1162 to 1242. He was an Imperial Vice-Councillor, *Gon-Chūnagon,* and the compiler of the *Hyakunin isshu,* "Single Poems by a Hundred Poets," from which over half of the poems in this book are taken. He assisted in the compilation of the *Shin Kokin Shū* for the retired Emperor Go-Toba, and the *Shin Chokusen Shū* for the Emperior Go-Horikawa, and left a diary, the Meigetsu-Ke, or "Bright Moon Diary." The translation is free—the Japanese refers to the "burning" sea water in the salt kilns.

SAIGYŌ (1118–1190) was descended from the Fujiwara. His secular name was Sāto Norikyo. He was a favorite of the former emperor Toba and a famous archer. At twenty-three he left his wife and children and became a monk and traveled throughout Japan reciting poetry and preaching. Saigyō inaugurates, with Shunzei and Teika, a new phase of the Japanese poetic sensibility.

LADY ŌTOMO NO SAKANOE lived at the beginning of the eighth century and she was the aunt of Ōtomo Yakamochi.

PRINCESS SHIKISHI (?–1201) was the daughter of the Emperor Go-Shirakawa. She became the princess of the Kamo Shrine in Kyoto, one of the principal shrines of Shintō. Later she became a Buddhist nun. She is one of the last of the great women poets of the Heian Court.

SHUNZEI'S DAUGHTER (1171–1252) is known by no other name. She was the sister of the great poet Sada-ie, known as Teika. Her father, her brother, Toshiyori, Toshimoto, and Saigyō the monk, were leaders of a revolution of the sensibility in the late twelfth century and first half of the thirteenth century. Shunzei is also known by the name he took when he became a Buddhist monk, Shaku-a. In those days there began a long period of civil wars that brought Heian civilization to an end.

MONK SOSEI, whose lay name was Yoshimine no Hironobu, lived at the end of the ninth century. He was the son of the Abbot Henjō.

LADY SUO was the daughter of Taira no Tsugunaka, Governor of Suo, and a Lady-in-Waiting of the Emperor Go-Reizei, who reigned in the middle of the eleventh century. The commentators give several legends, all improbable, about the occasion of the poem.

MIBU NO TADAMI lived in the tenth century.

MIBU NO TADAMINE lived in the tenth century. This poem has often been considered the best of the *Kokin Shū,* of which Tadamine was one of the compilers. His dates are sometimes given as 867–965.

FUJIWARA NO TEIKA (Sadai-e) (1162–1241) was the son of the poet Toshinari. He was involved in the gathering of the *Shin Kokinshu* and the *Hyakunin Isshu*

(*100 Poems of 100 Poets,* played as a card game to this day) and author of the introduction to *Superior Poems of Our Time* (*Kindai Shuka*), a critical landmark in the history of Japanese poetics. He and the poets associated with his poetics altered the course of Japanese poetry and changed the poetic sensibility. He is one of the major Japanese poets, though often considered decadent by the followers of the pure *Manyōshū* tradition. His most poignant love poems were written, as was *Hajime yori,* to young girls in his old age.

MINAMOTO NO TŌRU (Kawara no Sadaijin) died in 949. He was Minister of the Left, *Sadaijin,* living in Kawara, a part of Kyoto. The poem is very elliptical in Japanese; another reading could be:

> *Some woman*
> *Has made my mind as*
> *Disordered as Michinoku*
> *Cloth, printed with tangled ferns.*
> *It did not get that way*
> *By itself.*

FUJIWARA NO TOSHIYUKI lived from 880 to 907. He was an officer of the Imperial Guard and a famous calligrapher as well as poet.

KI NO TSURAYUKI (882–946) is a major poet of his period. He was general editor of the second anthology, the *Kokinshu,* and wrote for it a famous critical preface which founded Japanese poetic aesthetics and which is still taught as a masterpiece of early prose. He compiled another anthology, the *Shinsen Shu,* and a selection from the *Manyōshū.* He also wrote the *Tosa Nikki,* the *Tosa Diary,* of a journey from Tosa where he had been governor, back to the capital—another masterpiece of early prose.

ŌTOMO NO YAKAMOCHI lived from 718 to 785. He was the son of Ōtomo no Tabito, whose poems in praise of sake are famous, and who was a Grand Councillor of State. Yakamochi himself became a *Chūnagon,* Senior Councillor of State, after a career as a general, courtier, and provincial governor. His family, which numbered several poets, was broken up after his death because of a crime of one of its members. His poetry is exceptional in the *Manyōshū* for its exquisite delicacy. Lady Sakanoe was an aunt and lover of Yakamochi.

YAMAKAWA TOMIKO (1879–1909) was born in a small village now part of Kohama, Fukui Prefecture, and graduated from Girls' High School in Osaka, which seems to have been one of the best secondary schools for women in its day. She studied for a year at Women's University in Tokyo, and married at twenty-one. Her husband died a few years later and she herself died at thirty, leaving one book, *Koi-Goromo* (*The Garment of Lovemaking*), written in collaboration with Yosano Akiko and Chino Masako. She and Akiko were both lovers of Yosano Tekkan and of each other. She is the "lily" of Akiko's and Tekkan's poems and Akiko is the "white lespedeza" and Takino, Tekkan's first wife, is "white hibiscus." The relations of these three women and Chino Masako with each other and with Tekkan were extraordinarily complex and intense.

YOKOBUE lived in the twelfth century. Near the temple of Giō and the other women is a small shrine to Yokobue, heroine of another brief but poignant episode in the *Heike Monogatari*. She was a servant to Kenrei Mon-in. *Yokobue* means flute player. Tokiyori, the son of a courtier, fell in love with her but his father forbade him to have anything to do with her as he had already planned an influential marriage for his son. Tokiyori shaved his head and became a monk. When she heard this, Yokobue went seeking him and wandered toward Saga (not the modern town) above the Oi River. Under the full moon, in the time of plum blossoms, she heard the voice of Tokiyori changing Sutras. Yokobue sent him a message but he turned her away and then went to the great Shingon Temple complex at Mt. Kōya. There he heard that she had become a nun. They exchanged poems and shortly afterward she died in Nara, but her shrine is in Arashiyama.

FUJIWARA NO YOSHIFUSA (804–872) was Minister of the Right, Prime Minister, and Regent from 858 to 872. His daughter Akiko became the wife and

Empress of Emperor Montoku and the poem is to her. The original says "beautiful flower" rather than "flower like beauty." Under Yoshifusa and Akiko the power and wealth of the Fujiwara clan greatly increased.

SHAMBHALA LIBRARY

The Art of War: The Denma Translation,
by Sun Tzu. Translated by the
Denma Translation Group.

Love Poems from the Japanese, translated by
Kenneth Rexroth. Edited by Sam Hamill.

Shambhala: The Sacred Path of the Warrior,
by Chögyam Trungpa. Edited by
Carolyn Rose Gimian.

Siddhartha, by Hermann Hesse.
Translated by Sherab Chödzin Kohn.

Tao Teh Ching, by Lao Tzu.
Translated by John C. H. Wu.

*When Things Fall Apart: Heart Advice for
Difficult Times,* by Pema Chödrön.